Sweet Devilry

Sweet Devilry

by

Yi-Mei Tsiang

OOLICHAN BOOKS
FERNIE, BRITISH COLUMBIA, CANADA
2011

Library and Archives Canada Cataloguing in Publication

Tsiang, Yi-Mei, 1978-
        Sweet devilry / Yi-Mei Tsiang.

Poems.

ISBN 978-0-88982-273-3

        I. Title.

PS8639.S584S94 2011   C811'.6   C2011-901491-2

We gratefully acknowledge the financial support of the Canada Council for the Arts, the British Columbia Arts Council through the BC Ministry of Tourism, Culture, and the Arts, and the Government of Canada through the Canada Book Fund, for our publishing activities.

Published by
Oolichan Books
P.O. Box 2278
Fernie, British Columbia
Canada V0B 1M0

www.oolichan.com

Cover design by David Drummond - daviddrummond.blogspot.com.

Printed in Canada on 100% post consumer recycled paper.

For my mother, Louise,
who makes all things possible.

CONTENTS

1.

May 12, 2005   11
Aubade   13
Ultrasound   14
Monitor   15
Test Perspectives +/-   16
We Bring Our Children Tobogganing   22
Testing gravity   23
I know you will make your own way in the world   24
Kingston Pen   25
Two   27
Starting Daycare   29
October   30
Hannah   31
How to dress a two year old   32

2.

How to Take Care of The Baby   37
Mother - A little book for women   38
Beginning our Home in Canada   39
The Canadian Mother's Book   40
Household Cost Accounting in Canada   41
How to take care of the father and the family   42
How to take care of the mother   43
Hansel and Gretel   45
Bluebeard's egg   46
Dancing   47
Little   48
Red Riding Hood   49

3.

Den Lille Havfrue 53

4.

The Cataraqui Street Verses 71
On Surrendering 78
Sophie *Needle Exchange Office* 85
Making dirt angels in Skeleton Park 86
Purple Balloon *To Jean-Paul, 1978-1985* 87
Rivers of blood 89
Winter house 90
Before you died: 91
Women who cry when they drive 92
The lists we make 93
A good death 95
Saline 96
Visit 97
Remains 98
Swim Lessons 99
Last Will and Testament 101

1.

MAY 12, 2005

Oh, the morning of your birth
and I am a gutted fish.
The one that swallowed a diamond ring
whole, pale belly split to reveal such
an unlikely wealth.

There's not much to do here.
The nurses bring toast,
baby, pills, baby.
Drugs thicken my tongue; words drop,
roll against slippers that lie
prone, hollowed.

The tender puff of flesh around
your eyes hushes the light.
The whole of you seems this way;
cocooned, body a bruise that
flinches at its own violent making.

What can we do but curl around each other,
learn fatigue by its slow pull,
the deepening sink into colour, your eyes
practicing the shift
of dusk's gray afterglow into
a night sky rubbed thin with city lights.

What can I tell you?

Learn a good latch, kiddo —
it pays to hold on
to someone you love.

And holler little one, holler
until you can trust that the echo
of your voice will be me,
bending to your hunger.

AUBADE

Light pulls at the curtains with unsteady fingers,
the palsied hand of the morning after,
the bleary-eyed denial of dreams.

Morning with its small cries,
open-mouthed birds, the day
and its rattling hunger.

Shake out your dreams,
the hours you spent dead.
The baby is up, your nightgown dripping
with milk.

Leave-taking is this:
cleave yourself in two
what's left is like love,
a heavy slumber, a blind bed-warmth
a half remembered ache
you tow behind you,
leaving a wake in the day.

ULTRASOUND

First glimpse of my daughter,
a grey cloud, shape twisting
within me, a storm about to rise.

Here she is, casual,
hands on her belly, a patient
in a waiting room; old magazines,
red plastic chairs.

Her head turns; she stares through
my skin at our probe, at the
technicians hands, sees us
like we see God, a shadow,
a pressure, and her heart-sound

gallops through the room
like an accusation
her face towards us,
and I wonder if my mother

saw the same; wide dark
depression of eyes and
the hollow space within herself.

MONITOR

Rooms apart, I can hear your breath
better than my own, can set my heart
by the soft tides of your sleep.

This listening is a part of me now,
stilling my own breath.

I can hear your dreams orbiting my own,
waking towards a moon that lays heavy with light:
a solitary body, forever pulled towards another.

TEST PERSPECTIVES +/-

+

You must be swimming now,
uterus big as a lake, nothing
but night sky and a distant
voice from the dock,
calling you in.

-

I was sure you were there,
felt you heavy as heat, could
have slaked my thirst by you,
never imagined this dry
road, asphalt leading nowhere.

+

And to think, this morning, drinking tea, brushing
crumbs into my cupped palm. Life
was blowing into you, like a sail
catching wind, and me walking through
the kitchen, my body an open sea.

+

9 days late and
everything is
starting to be about
numbers.
Addition,

Subtraction.

+

Your first hello.

You slipped into me as quiet
as love, and you'll leave
as painfully.

But for now, you, without
a name, or body, simply
two lines,

where there were
none before.

+

You, my monthly succession
of +'s, each one small
as a torso, arms of a
hangman, and so far
I keep getting the letters
wrong.

Like Christmas,
a bit of a let-down.

Oh thank God.
I'll never date
him again.

It's like a telegram,
terse, without punctuation
and I'm not sure
if I'm ready to open it.

‐

That small pink line
thin as a filament vein,
empty of blood.

+

I think, that it might be
just you and me,
now kiddo.

+

No wonder
I've been throwing up.

+

Sweet thing, little thought,
I love you enough
to meet you again
in a couple of years —

Wait for me.

+

We called you into being,
plucked you out like a star,
a bright light in that dark space
only now do I realize
the size of the sun that's hurtling
towards us.

I can hear you,

the thin note of a reed

the sharp whistle of air.

+

It doesn't seem right, news
in a bathroom. Where are the trumpets,
the banners? Just us two, a toilet
and tiles, the first room in which
we exchange names.

+ + + +

All lined up
like crosses on a road,
each bearing a body.

+

I feel nothing
yet. Like watching
October snow,
those fat crystals,
melting in
mid-
air

WE BRING OUR CHILDREN TOBOGGANING

after wrestling with boots and mitts

after packing hot chocolate, teddy grahams, extra socks,
after waiting out the held-breath tantrum over zippers.

We stand at the top, an impasse, clouds of breath
forming a storm over their little woolen-wrapped heads.

Their voices needle us, sharp and small
— *I don't wanna* — enough to draw blood.

I hear the whir of a distant bird, air
plunging through its struggling wings.

Some days this is what it is to be a mother; wingless, a cliff,
and the choice to push or jump.

TESTING GRAVITY

You sleep with your arms extended, a surrender;
hands just reaching the top of your head
as though staving off crows;
the crush of a world where
everything towers above.

You spend your days testing gravity,
the proverbial apple and the highchair,
learning that everything has its own
way of falling.

Those hands, held up
even in your sleep,
remind me of your toddling accent,
your newfound words,

too much, mama

tired from pushing against the
ponderous weight of my love,
the fear
that it might topple.

I KNOW YOU WILL MAKE YOUR OWN WAY
IN THE WORLD

And still we do all those things that parents do,
bent back, teaching about bunnies and trees,
about how to knot ourselves and how one
pull can loosen everything, unbind us.

We show you a thousand ways of leaving us,
practice our goodbyes with brave faces,
teach you to let go of night's ledge,
fall into sleep in your own, narrow bed.

And yet I cannot learn my own lessons,
my heart which seizes at her like
a stranger in a van, the greedy love with
which I could smother her.

I had a friend who told me children prepare us to die
and I see now, how he was right,
how letting go is a kind of leaving, and

I know you will make your own way in the world.

KINGSTON PEN

Driving past the prison,
red turrets and limestone,
set on the edge of water
my daughter nearly leaps
from her car seat *Look
mommy! A castle!*

There could easily be
a beast inside,
a hidden prince.

We talk about prison
in terms of time-outs
and I know she pictures
small boys, unkempt hair,
the remains of snot drying
across their flushed cheeks.

All sitting on stiff backed chairs,
their legs kicking out the seconds left
on their time.

She's right — I've worked in prisons
before, seen the boys with metal shard
eyes, the large hands, the sloped shoulders.
Each with the mouth of a child,
raw and covetous.

I put her to bed under glowing stars,
a cloud of mosquito netting.
And I think of these men, murderers
a short jog from our home,
caught in the closed-fist sleep of children,
floodlights winking like stars.

TWO

She beats the linoleum, fists blooming
with blood under skin, a trapped scream.
Her legs fly out, each one straight as
a military march, flipping her torso
with their unmatched gait.

Her anger drags at me,
the rigid limbs, the stutter of teared breath
each cry a half word, vowels torn
between belly and throat.

I could watch this forever,
my hands loose, empty.
There's a sweet lethargy that fills me

as she jolts and shudders
into exhaustion, face pressed into
the kitchen floor, stray
crumbs crawling her
twitching arms like ants.

I sit at the table while
she sleeps hard for an hour,
try to summon love
as her body unclenches,
breath loosens to a sigh.

When she wakes, she reaches for me,
says *Dance*
collapses against me,
hair still a humid storm
face hot with sleep.

So we dance,
curled around each other
like lovers, the sweet croon
of a woman's voice,
and rain on the windows,
falling all around us.

STARTING DAYCARE

It's just a stage, this fear
that makes my daughter cling,
her love an electric charge; I hold
her hand, a current bridged between us,
while I pee. Her body shakes with its magnet
pull, her sobs echo in this stall
of our separation, and

it's just a stage, this violent
anger that rips through her,
flurry of fists a scatter-bomb,
her convulsing rage a God
who speaks in tongues, and

it's just a stage, this waking
into her own scent of sweat,
the sour-milk and clove
of her soaked sleepers. The cry
that floats across the dark upstairs hall
like a searchlight, looking to crash
against hard rock, and

it's just a stage, my heart
that lurches and betrays me,
as I pry her off, hand her
to a stranger; turn away.

OCTOBER

Every year we are blindsided
by the geese and their betrayal,
the milkweed's sudden loss,
breath of seeds exhaled,
orphans to the wind.

We pick the seeds from our sweaters,
the peeling paint from the doorway.
The lawn is a cold morgue preserving
the fallen bodies of leaves.

There is nothing but doubt in October,
and a dogged, worn faith. They are
the sky and the geese, the call and our
chilled silence. My daughter, on a bed
of leaves, as though she has fallen
from the sky. *Bury me, mommy,*
and she spreads her arms, a crucifixion,
a faith, that anything can rise again.

HANNAH

Hannah, the day we met your mother already glowed with you,
a heavy burden of light, a star still galaxies away,
and that small glimmer, your first language,
seeping through the pores of her.

Those beginning weeks, tucked tightly into a pouch,
your milk breath light as pollen, we took
you everywhere, planted poppies and peonies
in garden beds, your heavy head
nodding against your mother's breast, your neck
a stem beneath those closed, bright flowers.

We passed you around at parties, each of us
huddled around a fire; we shared you like a good bourbon,
the way you poured into our arms,
hot and sweet, made us dizzy
with the fullness of the world.

And, oh Hannah, that smile, that dandelion of a smile,
tiny bright suns in a field that can barely contain them,
seeds parachuting into other people's lawns.

HOW TO DRESS A TWO YEAR OLD

Practice by stuffing jello into pants.
Angry jello.

speakveryquicklywithoutbreathing
untilyoubegintoseeplanets
spinninglike
coinspirouetting
silverflashesof
light
and
balance

Write a blog post against the hegemonic practices of the
fully-dressed elite.

Threaten wildly and unpredictably:

Deliver Mr. Potato Head's
ear in an envelope

Froth at the mouth.

Be still.
Hold your words in the palm of your hand,
like birdseed. Let her small bones alight
on you with the hesitant uplift of almost-flight.
Make your hand the earthen weight of gravity.

Promise monkeys.

Slice your words into
The.　　Anger.　　Of.　　Pauses.

Quote random passages of Kafka.
It will buy you time.

Forbid her to wear clothes. Dress the dog in her favourite shirt.

Petition city hall to have the by-law officer enforce all
non-nudity legislation.

Issa said:

>   Children imitating cormorants
>   are even more wonderful
>   than cormorants.

Here she is, a cormorant, gleaming by the window's lake-light,
shirt closing tight as a snare around her throat.

2.

HOW TO TAKE CARE OF THE BABY

*"As in other occupations, a study must be made of this
occupation of bringing up the baby. You need to learn the
rules and the skill of it. Like every other business, it is
simple—when you know."* [1]

Hear that, little bird? It's simple,
this business of growing you.
Open wide – the abracadabra
of breast, mouth, milk; the secret
code of thrive.

But I've forgotten the password, can hear only in those
dream-echoes of my lost and wandering sleep; see the flit
of its nightshirt falling, rumpelstiltskin-style, through earth,
and then it's spelunking, always under-foot, the rat scabble
sound drawing you close with its manic, peekaboo promises
of sleep, never mind the perchance to dream.

Now.
Boil and iron the diapers.
Scald your hand into a charred wakefulness.
Don't forget to close the oven door.
Gingerbread and babies are known to wander.

---

1   The little blue books household series, publication No 3,
    issued by the Department of Health, Canada, 1923 pg 6

MOTHER - A LITTLE BOOK FOR WOMEN [1]

Table: A.

Before the baby was born. Lives lost Because of:	
Exhausted with care of children and home	67
Exhausted for want of Sleep and Rest	27
Exhausted from too frequent pregnancies	26
Poor	68

It boils down to the same thing,
exhausted for want
of a moment, alone with your own body,
not dripping, pushing,
or otherwise draining.

I knew of a woman, up from her birthing bed,
uterus still grasping at what
it had lost, steam billowing
from her skirts —

mending the fence as if it
were no more than another
rip, a light fabric too thin
to keep out the cold,
the wolves scenting for blood.

---

1   The little blue books national series, publication No 38,
    issued by the Department of Health, Canada, 1928 pg 8

BEGINNING OUR HOME IN CANADA

"There are some other things in regard to the duties of married life which could be whispered into your ear, but you would not want us to print them here." [1]

That first night, his hands the shy
muzzle of a soft-mouthed animal,
awkward grace.

In the morning, bread crumbles
at his touch, the cow sings
with relief, and I sweep the sheets into
the wind, hands still blushing
with the raw exertion of the wash.

At lunch, the afternoon sun laid
bright on the table where we eat hesitantly,
and I am surprised by the thinness of his wrists,
the shallow bones of a boy, still growing
into his hands.

Later, he tucks seeds tight into their bed of black earth,
hums prayers I have never heard.
Small words that take to the sky
and die in the open air.

I see him, from the kitchen window,
watch his bent back.
He works steadily away from me,
his body growing smaller until he is no larger
than a small cup.

---

1   The little blue books home series, publication No 7, issued by the
    Department of Health, Canada, 1923 pg 20

THE CANADIAN MOTHER'S BOOK

"At night, summer and winter, let the fresh air enter your sleeping-room." [1]

Hours since the doctor left,
lifted her small body,
velvet tufted head
no larger than his palm.

And still the curtains kick at the air
like lungs, fill out towards
the room and strain against
the screen, breath twisted
in sheets.

The nursery is already losing
her mark, wind lapping away at
her soft milk-fed smell,
smoothing the bed
where she died, sleeping.

I can hear the rest of the children,
shooed out of the house, scattering
into the open air, dust from a carpet.

They play warily, wedge themselves
into small spaces, the rotted trunk of an oak,
the rafters in the barn, their hearts
straining like caught birds.

---

1   The little blue books mother's series, publication No 1, issued
    by the Department of Health, Canada, 1923 pg 21

HOUSEHOLD COST ACCOUNTING IN CANADA

"Mother...in making the home and therefore the nation,
bearing and rearing the children, cherishing the good,
preventing the evil...needs from the Father and the Family
both love and money." [1]

What to do with my pin-money?
Finger-worn folded papers,
the merry jangle of a possibility

beyond corn syrup and barley meal:
Hide it. Hide it beneath the swarthy
late winter carrots, under the sink, or
between the rags and the righteous smell
of vinegar.

Let it ripen with spring bulbs,
swell like my daughter's budding
breasts, the skin's hidden wealth of
dark and burgeoning secrets.

When I bend to add the week's unspent change,
a clandestine meeting,
lean my ear to that rich, heavy jam jar
I hear the sticky whisper of
another life, a sweet defiance.

---

1 The little blue books household series, publication No 16,
   issued by the Department of Health, Canada, 1923 pg 36

HOW TO TAKE CARE OF THE FATHER AND THE FAMILY

"Are his feet wet? Give him dry socks and slippers. He is the Head of the Family and the Chief of our Strength." [1]

I like the feel of warm wool,
as though the socks were freshly shorn.
They wait by the fire,
full of the comfort that only
a thick soup and knit perl can offer.

I can measure the length of your day
by your socks, feel the heifers' reluctance
in the worn heel; the weight of your body
leans on that left crescent, worry eroding
yarn through the burden of light, dry skies,
gossamer clouds too sheer to net the rain.

I keep a basket full of wool worn bare —
each heel hemmed with soft,
practiced strokes, the delicate art
of binding back your loosening threads.

---

1   The little blue books household series, publication No 6,
    issued by the Department of Health, Canada, 1923 pg 7

HOW TO TAKE CARE OF THE MOTHER

*"Secondly, you have thought about other people's tastes so long
and so hard, that you scarcely know what you do like yourself.
Now! Now! If you like parsnips, have them — and let the
others have their turnips if they want them."* [1]

Lord, has it come to this?
I can barely remember what it is to taste;
my tongue an underfoot child
to the hard mechanics of those hassled,
distracted teeth.

Still, parsnips or turnips?

Wash the dishes and watch
early summer and the children,
scouring the grass, wild strawberries
bleeding from their feral jaws.

Those berries, each one smaller
than the half moon fingernail
of a new-born. A sweetness
that doesn't fill.

Turn the potage on the stove
watch the roots decay
into broth, an all-day
fullness of simmer and starch.

---

1   The little blue books household series, publication No 4,
    issued by the Department of Health, Canada, 1923 pg 6

At night, sit at the scrubbed table,
listen to the house soothe itself
by the sleep-heavy breath of children.
Watch tomorrow's bread heave and stir
with its yeasty dreams —
inching its growth with the unnatural
speed of youth.

Sit and savour the thought
of her small fingers, in from the fields,
the red blush stain popped in my mouth
the sweet of her, the salt that lingers.

HANSEL AND GRETEL

There was a reason
she sent those children to me.
Their father, a woodcutter
who would creep into their bedroom
at night, eyes glinting like an axe,
looking at all he could cut through.

She walked on that sharpened blade,
served milk, thinned with water,
saw how he trembled as their throats
moved, his hand blistering as he
stroked the scrubbed pine table.

The children came to me, their
hands like sparrows, they picked
shingles and chewed the tar
like licorice, opened their black
mouths to show me its sweetness.

I pitied them, swept the small
breadcrumbs from their pockets,
poured meat into their quavering throats.

But still their fingers felt
like hollow bones, light and brittle;
chalk about to crumble.

I turned to fire the oven for bread
and they were gone, into the dark woods;
called by the sound of their father felling trees.

BLUEBEARD'S EGG

I gave you a poison to carry, a bluebeard's egg,
and that small, locked, attic door.
You're too young for fairy tales. I can still pocket
the skeleton keys, bar the stairs, spend nights
pacing the hallway

thinking — a bucket of blood
seven wives torn to shreds

or you, in anaphylactic shock
bees in your throat,
and that sound of wings beating
air in a closed, swollen hive.

DANCING

Our daughter has left us.
Her fever opened the trap door
into that dark world, the boat
that glides to another shore.

We wait behind the door,
watch her body, pale and shaking,
flushed legs twitching
in a forced dance.

When she returns to us
exhausted, I want to shake her
demand where she's been,
seal the door where she slipped out.

For the first time, I feel for the king,
his jealous heart, his impossible orders.
He had seven daughters disappear,
his hands full of worn silk,
the body-warmth escaping
the scraps left of his daughters.

LITTLE

The sky fell the day you were born.
I was picking up the shards, and you
in your bassinet, sucked on a piece of cloud,
mist leaking down your chin.

I wanted to tell the king, you know, sky falling and all
but we brushed it into a corner,
birds pecking through the remains.

We still have some, the folded edge of a horizon,
tucked into your baby book,
a footnote to your birth.

RED RIDING HOOD

Alone, in the dark woods
or a street, a car stalks
shadow, a wolf's dark mouth.

There, the outline of a
body of leaves. Now she walks
alone, in the dark woods

of cement and dandelions, a bouquet
of yellow faces. A child's sidewalk chalk
shadow, a wolf's dark mouth

and the car, idling, plastic bags blown astray,
wind at her hood, the scream of a hawk
alone in the dark woods

of opened doors. Her mother would say
strangers,don't talk to them, don't you talk
shadow, a wolf's dark mouth

around her heart, beat quickened
and *hush* now, don't you talk
alone, in the dark woods
shadow, a wolf's dark mouth.

3.

"When we cease to exist here we only become the foam on the surface of the water. We have not immortal souls, we shall never live again...Human beings, on the contrary, have a soul which lives forever." Bedstemoder

"At every step you take it will feel as if you were treading upon sharp knives, and that the blood must flow...And if he should, the first morning after he marries another your heart will break, and you will become foam on the crest of the waves." Hav Forhekse

— Hans Christian Andersen
(1836)

DEN LILLE HAVFRUE

It was never about the man.
His pale face, his heavy sinking bones,
and that delicate breath, life rising like light
to meet the surface of the water.

I don't know what moved me to save him.
Human deaths seem so real.

Imagine ours. The slow

               siren alarm of

         your body every pore
             closes tight as a mollusk

             until each collapses, watch your

                 chest fall into an ocean,

      the soft breast of foam,

       itself.

Love is finite.

It's the end of every legend,
standing on the shore,
turning to look back at the sea and
crumbling like pillars of salt,
foam dissolving:

Faith requires a choice.

There are no words in our language
for this final moment.
It's enough to witness
each death, each one leaving
nothing but light and water:

Faith requires a question —

or at the very least, the absence of an answer.

There is little to trade
but my body,
or parts of it.

She cuts off my tongue,
blood unwinds
from my mouth
like so many ribbons.

The draught cleaves me,
clean as a knife,
legs bright and pale
as the moon, each step
trailing blood.

You don't know desire.

He finds me,
drying in the sun,
legs soft as jellyfish.

Winds his arm around my waist,
clucks his tongue like a nursemaid
and carries me up his marble steps,
shoulders hunched protectively over me,

                              I'd like to step into him,
                    pull his hard body over me, like a shell.

How do you make a man love you
without words?

It's not as easy as you would think.

Mute, I am his foundling,
that sweet dumb beast who follows
and sleeps curled at his door.

I'm too close to this role,
silent, loyal, nothing to offer but
my large wet eyes,
heavy breath,

      an unspoken plea.

His dog is unnaturally fond of me,
tries to lick my legs into submission,
winds his small body between my feet.

We can sense our own
limited time.

I lied.

It was about the man.

At least partly, at least in the beginning.
You see, he smelled like sand in the afternoon. Like the sun
had licked him dry and left nothing but fine pebbles,
the sculpture of a man.

His hand could hold the whole small of my back.

I was fifteen.

Of course I loved him.

We would sit on marble, legs in the ocean
when everyone else was sleeping.

He would hold my feet, flex the toes,
stroke the arch until I wanted to weep
with the pain.

It was dark enough that he couldn't see
my eyes, couldn't read that mute agony.

Instead, his eyes would hold the ocean,
the shudder of waves
creeping closer, as if he called it,
as if it answered.

All those nights in the warm salt air,
my legs draped across him,
the tide's warm rhythm
and the pull of the moon;
his hands never strayed.

I hated him too.

There's another woman.

A wife   to be.

I imagine her

eyes a dark chalice, something he can pour himself into, feel religious about.
A mouth that is all tongue and teeth, words that drop lithely to the ground, sentences cut cleanly with those neat, even teeth.

He will meet her soon. Sails are set and the body of the ship climbs awkwardly over waves — we sit together in the cabin and watch the vessel tremble, his arms wooden and damp against my back.

Splinters climb me.

Oh God.

She's like the sun seen from the ocean, a purple flower, light streaming from the calyx.

She's the one who found him first, after I dragged him to shore, his thin ribs still heaving the ocean's storm.

Finders keepers.

There's no need for weeping, door slamming,
the loud grief normally needed for the end
of a hopeless first love.
There isn't time.

He'll marry her tonight,
and the slaves are dancing,
each spinning in gold and red scarves
like a trailing scream.

I dance for them too,
the smiling bride, the exquisite prince:

I am a fury of motion, each light step
brilliant in its pain, each elegant anklet
a silver voice, calling.

He beckons me,
strokes my hair fondly, kisses a strand
and turns to his betrothed.

Even now, I can't turn away from him.

The moon is dissolving.

My sisters' heads part the water's reflection,
the sound of light falling,
small drops on marble steps.

They are both bald, scalps bleeding,
their eyes darker against these pale crowns.

The knife they hold is for his heart.

My sisters.

I cried out for their hair,
those poor raw scalps.

The sound that came
was like a sea bird, strangled
in fishing wire.

These few poor words,
caught at the base of
my stunted tongue.

It's now that I grieve.

They whisper the terms:

Let his blood wash your feet,
claim the life that leaves him.

Return to us.

I weep into their cold skin,
harsh, loud tears.

They push me away —
looking to the east, the threat
of an early sun.

Point their thin fingers
to the steps and tell me

grieve him

The room resounds
with their quiet,
entwined breath.

Her hair fades into the pillow,
golden roots shifting with sea air
a feather of it blown to land,
possessively, across his chest.

They are both so still
that only the air moves
them, adjusts a hair,
blows gently on the underside
of her delicate neck.

They are a hushed breath,
                              waiting.

Already the sky is lightening
to a mute grey, the stars receding.

I saved his life.
Held those thin ribs
and surfaced to a storm.

I've lost my grip.
The ocean has calmed
and we're back to this:

You, my dear, the long breath of sleep
and the certainty that one of us will die.

Do you remember reading Hamlet to me,
both of us curled on your couch,
your soft palms gathering
my soundless tears?

Dream, my love.

Morning breaks;

light slices a horizon.

4.

THE CATARAQUI STREET VERSES

Moving In

Four back-breaking washing machines
to lift, and not a dryer in sight.

So goes our backyard, newly bought
and I swear, they lifted anything metal
and brought it here, to rust,
the previous tenants perched in the house,
watching rain eat away the sides.

Picture them:
roosting in the dank of the house like crows,
the smell of wet leaves, mold,
and couches bowing to their weight
like branches.

*

The garage stood tall as a barn,
sweet with the smell of honey,
rotting wood.

The day we demolished it
a hive fell, protected
under two pieces of debris.
We found it later, clearing the site:
split in two, paper rustling like
a book before fire.

*

We peeled the house,
lifted carpet until the dust
clung in thick grey sheets
against the windows,
like black-out curtains
during war-time.

Under the carpet we found wood
the smooth dark gold of amber ale, pine
planks near a hundred years old,
knots winking up knowingly.

Getting To Know The Neighbours

"Nice garden" says the man with prison
tattoos as he strolls past, the green tear
drop hanging off his face
like a drop of water
from my garden faucet.

*

At the baseball diamond near our house
people cart in their beer, drugs, lounge in the
stands and curse at imaginary players, lost lovers
cut their words across our yard —
Fucking cunt lighting up the sky,
blue bursting at the seams.

*

The glass balls that my neighbours put up,
small bubbles above their gate,
held on by the spider string of fisher's line

turning with the wind, baubles,
pretty as wampum.

*

We find a pair of shat-on men's underwear
sitting in the back of our yard,
casually, as though its always been there,
as though its not embarrassed by its own
telling state.

*

The newly sold house across the street is dipped
in lime greens, oranges bloom wildly
across the walls and all we can think is
thank Christ, it's not the creamy
beige of rentals.

*

The *click tap thwack* at 3 in the morning
is the broken stutter of
a left heel, snapped off,
and a local girl, still working,
making her way down to dark brick
of the woolen mill.

*

After the underwear, we built a fence
and still my daughter slides to the tune of their arguments
feet landing at the same time that another man
goes down, nose broken,
bits of blood showing through the
peek-a-boo slatted fence.

It's A Beautiful Day In The Neighbourhood

If you were, say, a stranger
to Kingston, looking at a map,
downtown would have soft edges,
a roundish amoeba slowly hulking
into larger forms.

If you were from Kingston
you would see the rigid spine
of the city, Princess St.,
south of which one might find
pillars and stained glass, shops entirely devoted to hats
and north of which one might find
shoes hanging like Christmas ornaments
from the power lines, soles suspended.

*

The tannery sits just north of us, on the edges of the water,
the factory's paint peeling off languidly
like an old man, picking away
at his psoriasis, raw flakes of the decay
sifting to the warehouse floor.

It's abandoned, although the stink
still lingers, death, the hot metal smell
of panic, and the dull clang of rain, old jokes.

*

City workers took down the baseball field's bleachers,
moms at Saturday night games now cheer from
summer grass, dads spreading windbreakers
over the dirt.

But the junkies, undeterred and ever
innovative, lift a picnic table,
place it in the brush behind the baseball diamond.
Small fires twinkle in the dark, the fireflies
of pipes or spoons.

*

The park west of us is built on a cemetery,
swings and slide well cemented
over thinly buried bones.

Every now and again,
a dog picks up a femur,
runs wild with the fine bones
of a lady's hand,
come to wave at the children.

This is not a metaphor.

Landscaping

Someone has fished out
a cart from the river,
left it lying in the dirt
like a decaying sun-fish,
gills turning a soft brown.

*

The Brown-Eyed Susans
are wide-eyed, necks twisted
and broken where a foot

has a fallen, needle
caught in their leaves,
the thin tip furrowing
into the earth's
yielding arm.

*

Cars slide the smooth sound
of whale song, the hum-shiver
lament, bridge the throat of
the Cataraqui river,
a single note,
beached.

*

Shopping carts are forever mistaking
our house — maybe it's the smell of bread,
or the call of canned beans.
Whatever it is, they sit on our lawn,
beseeching with the silent accusation
of all strays.

Development

Large orange machines roll in,
filled with a developer's confidence.
Simple, small gestures
turn the earth, toxic sludge.
The remains of tanning
are swept clean, the excavator a
busy housewife in spring.

Next summer a row of condos
will spring up, like tall red saplings,
rooted to the river
and reaching towards the sun.

*

The house, revalued,
leans south
like a dog straining against a leash,
like the keenly thrust hand of a social climber.

*

We find blankets and a pillow in the brush
behind the soccer field, stuffing molded
from an autumn of rain. The blankets
are thrown aside, as though the owner
woke suddenly, surprised by a bed
without a house.

ON SURRENDERING

It's true what they say about women. Waving that white flag
so handily; a skirt, a handkerchief, linens blowing across
enemy lines. Our bodies taught us this art of surrendering,
loosened us so we could let go of

blood
milk
children

There is a limit to what can be born.

Let your fist fall open, lie back: know that this child needs
so much more than blood,
and that small space to

dream bone, sinew, first muscle.

Breathe

and hold within yourself
a place for him – a burrow, warm, dark and large
enough to contain a name, a nest of bark, the almost-heat
of your body: a place deep enough

for a torpid winter's sleep.

Then let him slip from your body.

It's true what they say about women.

Our bodies taught us this art of surrendering,
loosened us so we could let go of

blood
children
milk

Learn what it means to have been left.

You staked your territory, embryo
flag planted
and the colonial demand for foreign customs, redrew
territorial lines of the body

(lungs,
spleen)

Made way for your growing empire.

Yes, there is an art to surrendering, to children, to bearing
that painful contraction, raw
unclenching and the held-breath push

of distance, separation,

so you can stand alone.

It's true what they say about women.

We can wave that white flag so handily;

let go of

                children
                milk
                blood

Learn how to carry

fear,
wrapped tight in cloth,
flecked with road-dust.

Those first months, ceding to your breath
            so light it could barely fill
your chest.

Ribs gray and thin as moth's wings,

and that same,

            hesitant hover:

not knowing what would smother you,
and closing my eyes

        to your small, perilous sleep.

SOPHIE
Needle Exchange Office

Sophie crushes dilaudid,
shapes soft powder with her hands,
spoons it over a flame until it has the fine-hair feel
of his warm scalp, hot and flushed with sleep.

She disappears after they take him.
I am afraid to walk home along the river, and find her
open-eyed, pupils dark with broken glass,
lungs bleeding with that seaweed taste
between last breath and a sky of water.

The last time I saw her I was pregnant,
thick ankled, rising like dough
in the summer heat of my office. Sophie held my waist,
let my child swim towards the dark sun of her palm.

When I see Sophie again my daughter Abby reaches
her hands to feel the craters of old abscesses
on Sophie's arms, frozen pools of dark blood.

Sophie holds my child easily, her mother-hands
cup round thighs, and I remember
what she told me about her own child —

the soft open-sky feeling of his head,
the dark down on his skin
stroking his back until dawn and holding the thought
of his shoulders, turning in the darkness inside her
wings that will fall softly, boneless
in first air.

MAKING DIRT ANGELS IN SKELETON PARK

Spring, and the dirt is dry as bones.
We are splayed here, dusting
our way under the swing set
our arms summoning sand storms.

My daughter is a small dirt angel,
pauper, cheek-smudged cherub.
Ten thousand souls
shift underneath us,
bones crumbling like chalk.

Each one feels the flutter
of her wings, the ocean of her
heart, pounding against them.

Every graveyard
should have a swing-set.

PURPLE BALLOON
— *To Jean-Paul, 1978-1985*

My daughter picks the balloon book,
a piece written by a hospice, about children dying.
We flip through the pages, my voice intoning
that "dying is hard work".
Her finger traces the puckered outline
of the purple balloon.

I suppose this is what gets me thinking
about you, Jean-Paul, your name always
the puff of last-run breath, that hard searing
cold that sits in your chest before you
can take another breath, the wet wool
taste of late afternoons, snow.

You had the half-grin of older boys,
your baby teeth crooked in your mouth
jostling for position — and the short,
harsh stubs of your hair, my first
raw longing.

I didn't go to your funeral,
imagined that you had skipped through the
ranks of childhood like a gifted kid,
conscripted to adulthood,
your cancer-light body shrouded
in the dark wool of a stiff suit.

All these years to mourn you, Jean-Paul
and it's not until I sit here, in a public library,
books laid bare and my daughter,
that same gentle curve of a child's cheek.

I feared the wrong thing.
Your grin, that halfways shine
heart-stopper: it grew
younger every year.

RIVERS OF BLOOD

It floods our city. It's coming through the taps — a stutter of rusty water and then the thick mass of blood rushing through the faucet like a cut artery. No one knows what to do. People don't want to get their shoes wet. We have placed towels against the sweep of the door. Each towel blooms red, fibers plumping with life. My daughter throws a box of band-aids out the window — we watch them float on the current like matchsticks. We sit on our roofs, waiting for FEMA, ears tuned to the thrum of helicopters. But no one comes. The sun stings our skin, dries us like scabs. The Church blames the gays. People are starting to point fingers, to ask *who* is bleeding. We look around, warily, all trying to hush the telling murmur of our hearts.

WINTER HOUSE

My father threw his language overboard,
a bag of kittens, waterlogged mewling:
small hard bodies.

My mother hung on to hers —
those slight words a thin web of frost
on the window, light melting the edges.

My daughter is starting to pick at language,
holds naming for dawn – *dog, star, mumma* —
alone in her crib, learning the edges that will mark
meaning, create borders.

I'm trying to find those words of my mother's,
the dust settling sound of *chien*, the sharp edged *étoile:*
words that become thick, undefined,
pulled from a soft mouthed *gueule.*

There is distance in words.
Translation a kind of poverty,
a thin house you can winter in,
cupboards arranged so you can never find a mug.

This is all I give you, Abby —
a measure of the distance
between you and your grandparents:
a cup of snow,
           a net dripping with sea.

BEFORE YOU DIED:

I said I would bear you water lilies to prove your passage, to blossom the moment of your last breath, a soundless explosion of sorrow and relief.

I inhaled you, forced the smell of your sun-warmed skin and antiseptics into my lungs, compressed you within my chest and promised not to exhale.

I said I was sorry I didn't make you more tea, but I would bury you in fragrant leaves, rosehips, bee balm, jasmine.

I didn't say anything, I drew pennies from your ear and held them so tightly they burned into my skin, collected heavy in my throat, a mouthful of copper; I could not speak.

I pressed dry lips to your long earlobe and tasted the salt of your body, a crystal bitterness that blooms in the darkness of deep sea.

I prayed in tongues, a supplicant to a vengeful god, as though your body would rain down rivers of blood and locusts, devour me.

I told you endless lies, stringing together stories, Arabian nights, and my voice never faltered through deserts or storms.

I held my hands for you to fill, your breath seeping like water between tightly pressed fingers.

WOMEN WHO CRY WHEN THEY DRIVE

"I held you for days in my heart, dear sad woman in the dark green Volvo"
    — Sue Goyette

Haven't we all done it? Legions of women driving and weeping, alone in that slim space of peace between where you were and where you'll be,

or who and what. And it's that road hum, I think, the tuneless breath of comfort that reminds of us of our mothers, our backs bared to them, their hands soaping and

throats humming in the way that their whole bodies once did, for us, the music of their rushing blood and breath, before we could know desire,

so complete were we then. And now, my friend, now on the long drawn breath of the 115, slender pines bathed in the tepid light of fall, passing them so that they drop

from view like needles, and my father ahead, wrapped in blankets, his bones drying like kindling, the split sound of cancer, driving home to clean the gutters,

rake the leaves, bundle the logs into neat packages against the brick, cords of wood unraveling into the fire.

THE LISTS WE MAKE

1. Diagnosis

Your bones had already hollowed,
my cheek rested on your thigh.
We listened to the wind's rush,
the oncoming violence.

2. *Resection*

Your body lay fallow,
blood and tendons turned.
The scalpel harvesting
earth, weeds, brittle hay.

You watched it all, or so you thought,
held by air warmed
under bright lights, multiple suns,
a killdeer abandoning a crushed nest.

3. *Convalesce*

We sat together, in our sunroom,
drank endless tea, joked
about the hole in your centre,
made lists of things to fill it:

gin, rosemary,
tin cutters, baby shoes,
jam jars,

until you settled on birdsong,
the shrill alarm of a magpie.

4. *Palliation*

You can't stand to be touched
barbs and quills pointed
into thin flesh.

Your frantic heart seizing air,
tries to pump through
bone, lungs, brain:

muscle twitch
of remembered flight.

A GOOD DEATH

Before your bones rose to meet your skin
and blanched under fluorescent hospital lights.

Before you pointed to the deer rib by willow,
entwined in a root that sank into its open chest
bone split like your arm rooted in tubes,
a forest growing despite you.

Before this, you sat with my head in your lap
braided my hair with apple blossoms
your fingers thick with the scent
of spring, of slender red twigs that
that bleed lush green when snapped over knee.

You made me promise you a good death, like this:
sitting with me, holding my hair
over your face.

SALINE

After he died we stormed the house
intent on scrubbing it clean of my father's cancer.
Garbage bags full of swabs, dressings, half-jars
of Vaseline. It was futile, really,
the hospital bed with its rails up,
as if it could prevent a fall.

I watched as my brother emptied
jar after jar of saline solution down the kitchen sink.
I'd never seen him like this;
how his back held his grief
straight and stiff, a shadow
pinned to the wall.

My mother had made the saline solution
every night, stacked jars to cool
in a large green wash basin on the counter.

It takes so little, I am overcome:
the jars, emptied and drying,
dividing the sunlight between them.

VISIT

I saw my father yesterday,
sitting on the wall of his mausoleum.
He held my hand and told me he forgave me
and I asked, for what?

He smelled of apples, an autumn of leaves
for skin. I remember you like this, I said,
a harvest -- an orchard of a man.

He opened his shirt, plucked a plum
from his lungs and held it out to me.
Everything, he said, is a way of remembering.

REMAINS

When I die, cremate me
and pour me into a mason jar:

Leave me by the toaster,
and let me get sticky with jam and toast crumbs.

Stack my ashes in the cellar
beside the pickled beets,
thick red bulbs suspended
like stilled hearts.

Or hang the jar from our maple.
Make me a windchime
let my loose teeth rattle
against the glass.

Listen.
All that remains
is the faint and cellared smell
of our skin, our small glass songs.

SWIM LESSONS

We're all here, clinging to babies.
Their unearthly warmth,
fat bikinied legs and swim diapers
a sodden and welcome heat.

The pert and buoyant instructor
tells us to dunk the unsuspecting tykes,
she prods truculent mothers
into proud and confident smiles,
convinced children are dumb as oxen --
obediently revising their expressions
from terror to a faraway peace
that comes only from really good cud.

And so we push our children, one by one;
force their heads below water.
Watch the bubbled cry surface
just before they do, arms milling in panic.

I hold my daughter, wait our turn,
and think of my father, morphine rolling
off his tongue, the carnivalesque wakeful
dreams that plagued him, trying to track
bubbles that crept up the hospital wall, hung
off the ceiling like diaphanous spiders,
spinning their own bodies into being.

He drowned in that room, black hair floating
in crisp white sheets and the smell of
chlorine. Each word came slow
and distorted, up from the
pool that gathered in his lungs.

Abby is underwater now, hair spread,
waving frantically, and there's
a moment when I freeze, hold her struggling
body against the rise of oxygen within her;
then scoop her out, her body rigid with rage.
Our eyes meet and I set my expression;
fear, pride.

LAST WILL AND TESTAMENT

To my husband, I leave the covers.

> The warm curl of space on the left of the bed,
> the autumn smell of my body, cloves and cinnamon.

To my friend Sheri, I leave the harvest moon.

> The thin psalms you once sang to it, the smoke-breath
> of watching night fall in a frosted field, stubbles of cut stalks
> written on the backs of your thighs, another kind of grief.

To my neighbour Kendra, I leave a collection of toys.

> Giraffes, horses, and dinosaurs, inch tall jungles of bright
> plastic light, the early morning shared sandbox, our hands
> trembling with coffee, children who were grown by noon.

To my brother, Francis, I leave our mother's ring.

> The 1/2 caret diamond set in gold, our parents before
> they were our own. The honeymoon in Peggy's Cove,
> spray of salt water against the smooth cold rock, the time
> before we understood erosion.

To Jane, my fellow poet, I leave my stubbornness.

> The stack of rejection notes, the ring of coffee stains
> on my writing desk. The secret that poetry is not literature
> but meditation, that poetry is not art, but a way to learn
> how to be in this world.

To my dog, Beijing, I leave mornings.

> Large, glossy mornings, the orange half-sun
> rising over the river, clouds of breath, the sharp
> edge of frosted grass which crunches like
> kibble under his hungry paws.

To my daughter, Abby, I leave the smoke of these memories:

> Creating language together, your small sounds rippling
> in the air between us, your tiny fists trying gather them back.

> The fall days we spent spinning into piles of leaves,
> like bright copper pennies clacking into the cracks of the
> sidewalk.

> The swing by Cataraqui River, your shoes flying into the sky;
> a flock of birds, your jealous feet.

> Goodnight moon, the sleep-heavy weight of your body,
> your mouth puckered and sucking as if my body
> had left you wanting.

Acknowledgements:

I'm grateful to the Ontario Arts Council for its support during the writing of these poems. Many of these poems have appeared in *CV2*, *The Antigonish Review*, *Other Voices*, *Cahoots*, *Room Magazine*, *Interimmag*, *Arc Poetry Magazine*, *Vallum Magazine*, and *Carousel*. Thank you to these editors. My gratitude also to the editors of Rubicon Press, who produced a broadside, "On Surrendering", and Leaf Press who created a chapbook, *The Mermaid and Other Fairy Tales*, from poems included in this book.

This manuscript has benefited from the keen eyes and insights of many great writers, especially Susan Musgrave (UBC), Helen Humphreys (Queen's Writer in Residence), Karen Connelly (Humber School for Writers), Anne Simpson, and Sheri Benning (BFF). Many of these poems came out from Susan's writing exercises, including "Visit", "I know you will make your own way in the world" and "Last Will and Testament". Eternal gratitude to Sheri Benning for her years of support and friendship; it was her book, Earth After Rain, that first opened my eyes to the possibilities and beauty of poetry.

Many thanks to the fellow students in UBC's MFA opt-res program, especially Tyler Perry for his feedback and impassioned midnight readings. My gratitude to The Villanelles: Kirsteen, Wayne, Sadiqa, Ashley, Heather and Jane. Your critics and friendship are invaluable.

Thank you to my husband, Tim McIntyre, who has helped me in every stage of my writing. Your edits and support have made me the writer I am. Your humour and love sustains me. And of course, thank you to Abby, my daughter and my joy.

Yi-Mei Tsiang is the author of *Flock of Shoes* (Annick Press, 2010) and *The Mermaid and Other Fairy Tales* (Leaf Press, 2010). She has two new books for children forthcoming with Annick Press. Her work has been sold and translated internationally. She has published poetry extensively in Canadian journals, and has appeared in several anthologies. She is currently completing UBC's MFA program, and works as a mentor to aspiring writers through UBC's Booming Ground and Queen's University's Enrichment Studies Department. Yi-Mei lives in Kingston with her husband and young daughter. She drew from her own experiences as a mother in the creation of the poems in *Sweet Devilry*.